Silver Burdett Picture Histories
The Days of Knights & Castles
1066–1485

Silver Burdett Picture Histories

The Days of Knights & Castles

Pierre Miquel
Illustrated by Pierre Probst

The Days of Knights and Castles
Translated and adapted by Penny Davies
from La Vie privée des Hommes: Au temps des chevaliers et des châteaux forts
first published in France in 1976 by
Librairie Hachette, Paris

This edition published in 1980 by
The Hamlyn Publishing Group Limited
London · New York · Sydney · Toronto
Astronaut House, Feltham, Middlesex, England

Published in the United States by
Silver Burdett Company, Morristown, N.J.
1981 Printing

ISBN 0-382-06472-0

Library of Congress Catalog Card No. 80-52502

Contents

Introduction

The Middle Ages are not easy to define. There was no definite beginning or end to the period as there is with a king's reign. Even historians disagree about the time-span of the era. Some believe that events in Italy mark the limits of the period, with the sack of Rome in AD 410 as the start and the Renaissance in the late fifteenth century as the finish of the Middle Ages. Not everyone takes this view. This book describes life and events between 1066 and 1485, a period all historians agree formed part of the Middle Ages.

Europe in the Middle Ages was a very different place to the Europe of the Common Market era. To begin with the countryside looked quite different. Very little of it was used, in comparison with today. Huge areas were covered by woods and forests thicker and denser than any that are left now. The area taken up by farmland was really quite small. England had a population of about three million before the Black Death struck in 1348, so large crop-growing areas were unnecessary.

No motorways or railways criss-crossed the landscape. In places the great roads built by the Romans were still used, otherwise a few poorly-made roads and rough tracks wound between the small, scattered towns and villages. Only the rivers looked much the same, except that the boats sailing up and down them were different. The rivers of Europe were probably as busy as they are today and the rivers of England were far more busy. And, because the cargo boats of the time were so much smaller than any commercial, cargo-carrying boats today, they could get much farther up the rivers, so that towns many miles from the sea were ports.

The countries of Europe were also quite different. In a period lasting as long as the Middle Ages there are bound to be changes of boundaries, as state fights with state for more territory. At the beginning of the period Europe was dominated by the Holy Roman Empire. Historians have described this state as being neither Holy nor Roman!

This is quite true as the empire covered what is now most of West Germany, the Netherlands, Austria, Switzerland and Italy as far south as Rome. The political importance of the empire entirely depended on the strength of the emperor. Men like Otto I, who was crowned in 962, and Henry III (1046–56) wielded enormous power, but if the ruler was weak the empire split up into a mass of semi-independent states.

There was no United Kingdom. England, Scotland, Ireland and Wales were separate countries at first (p. 48) and English kings had as much land in France as in England. When Henry II died in 1189 his territory in France covered Normandy, Brittany, the Auvergne, Anjou and south to the Pyrenees. In contrast, the king of France only had land in Flanders, Champagne, Burgundy and Toulouse. By 1360 the English lands in France had become smaller, but a lot of France was still under English control. Indeed, not until 1450 did English kings give up their claims to French territory, apart from the port of Calais. France itself had many strong, independent nobles, for example the dukes of Burgundy. These men were like kings in their own huge lands, and if the French king was weak, these men were really very much more powerful.

Spain was occupied for the early part of the period by the Moors (p. 49). But, gradually, they were driven back until they remained only in Granada, and the rest of what is now modern Spain was dominated by the Christian kingdoms of Castile, Leon and Aragon. By the sixteenth century, when these kingdoms had united into one, Spain had become one of the most powerful countries in Europe.

Building of some important cathedrals begins:

Albi: 1282	*Canterbury: 1096*	*Milan: 1387*
Amiens: 1220	*Chartres: 1194*	*Paris: 1163*
Autun: 1120	*Dublin: 1213*	*Poitiers: 1166*
Avila: 1160	*Ghent: 1274*	*Rheims: 1211*
Beauvais: 1230	*Laon: 1160*	*Rouen: 1201*
Bourges: 1200	*Limoges: 1273*	*Wells: 1170*
Burgos: 1222	*Lincoln: 1192*	*Winchester: 1079*

A knight's ideals:

To be brave and loyal
To be faithful to his king
To defend the Christian faith
and the Church
To protect widows and orphans,
the old and the weak

Italy did not become the united country we know today for many centuries after the Middle Ages, indeed it was not until 1871 that Italy was finally unified. Early in the period the region was more or less divided between the Kingdoms of Naples and Sicily in the south, and the Papal States and the Holy Roman Empire in the north. By the fifteenth century the power of the empire had declined so much that the north of Italy had become a collection of city states. The most important of these were Florence, Venice and Milan, although states like Mantua or Parma might become powerful for a short while if they had a particularly strong ruler.

Life in medieval Europe was often a struggle. Famine was a real problem and disease a constant threat. There was little time for recreation or leisure activities. That is why there is almost no medieval art, literature or music that is not religious. The non-religious or secular arts, like some music and literature were enjoyed by a few rich people. Art of any kind to glorify God was quite acceptable, in fact it was important to do the best possible work in praise of God. But art as a way of expressing oneself was an idea few medieval people would have understood. This was for the very practical reason that time and energy were best spent getting a living. And, because getting a living was not easy, there was neither time nor energy left for anything much else.

Most people throughout Europe lived in villages, perhaps with as few as ten houses. Unless there was a market town nearby where they could sell any excess produce, most villagers never left the place where they were born. There was really no reason to go

Studies and examinations:

Secondary education covered three main subjects known as the trivium: Latin grammar, rhetoric and logic. Rhetoric was the art of public speaking and debating, logic was the art of reasoning.

After successfully studying these subjects students learn the quadrivium: music, arithmetic, geometry and astronomy.

At university a student chose his special subject: law, theology, medicine. After seven years' study he could qualify as a Master of Arts and could teach. But to be a Master of the University he had to be a Doctor of Letters. When he received his degree, the new Master of Arts was also given a special cane with a disk on the end. This was to be used to smack his students' hands if they misbehaved in any of his classes.

The chief currencies of Europe in 1350:

The gold florin of Florence
The silver livre of France
The gold ducat of Venice
The gold penny of England

The population of Europe in 1328:

In 1328 France covered 424,000 square kilometres and had approximately 3,370,000 families. This gave a population density of 7.8 families per square kilometre – the highest in Europe. Holland and the Kingdom of Naples both had populations nearly as big. England had a population of about 3½ million and Italy between 8 and 10 million. The population of Germany and Eastern Europe was never properly estimated.

anywhere else. Because communications were so poor, villages were almost entirely self-sufficient, so there was no need to go shopping, even if there was any money to spend and *that* did not happen very often. Families lived in the same village for generations, so there were no relatives in different places to go and visit. Tombstones in old churchyards give a good picture of this. The same few surnames appear again and again, even centuries after the Middle Ages were definitely over.

Towns had been few and far between in the early Middle Ages. They had also been of little social or economic importance. But with improved communications and increasing trade their influence began to grow. Until, by the end of the period, they had achieved an importance they have never since lost. Certainly in England, the Middle Ages marked the beginning of the end of an entirely rural society and economy. This change is underlined by two representatives from each town being summoned to the meetings of the Great Council of Edward I (1274–1307).

If, after reading this book, you think that the Middle Ages were a dirty, uncomfortable period and the people believed some extraordinary things, stop and think. What about pollution, traffic jams, nuclear contamination and the many people who believe in flying saucers, UFOs and the Loch Ness monster!

The plague in England:

1348 About one-third of the population died
1360 Some 22% died
1369 Some 13% died
1375 Some 12% died
1665 The last outbreak of the plague in England

Severe famines in Europe:

1314–16 Flanders and north-west Europe
1333 Catalonia (north-east Spain)
1335–37 Languedoc (south-east France)
1340 Italy

Tolls paid at Bargate, Southampton, September 1439:

9 half bales of woad – 4p; 2 tuns (barrels) of oil – 17p; 1 pipe of oil – 3p; 4 quarters of malt – 1p; 1 pipe of oil and 3 half bales of woad – 4½p; 5 half bales of woad and 1 barrel of lard – 3½p.

Life in a Village

In the Middle Ages most people lived in small country villages. The chief towns, like London, Paris or Madrid, were no bigger than a large modern village. In 1377 London only had a population of 35,000 and York, the second city of England, had 11,000 inhabitants. In 1300 Edinburgh only had 400 houses. Compare that with the size of a large modern housing estate!

Each village was an almost self-sufficient community, with a fairly rigid social structure. At the top was the landlord or lord of the *manor*. The farm-lands belonged to him and if he was very wealthy he often had many villages and estates. A *bailiff* helped him run them. Next came the village craftsmen – the blacksmith, the carpenter, the wheelwright and the miller. Then there were the rest of the villagers – the serfs or *villeins*. Each family farmed some of the estate land, paying rent in return. The rent was seldom paid in money. Instead, it was paid in time and produce, as the account book of a Norfolk estate shows. In 1272 Hervey de Monte, who rented 18 acres, paid for it with 4 hens, 3 half days of weeding on his lord's land, 1 day's ploughing for the lord and 3 days' carrying grain to the barn at harvest time, among other tasks. If a tenant upset his land-lord his land could be taken away and given to someone else.

Countries were run in the same way. At the top was the king, the chief landlord. He gave huge estates to a few noblemen. In turn they gave some of this land to less important men and so on down to the villeins. The nobles paid for their estates by sending their landlord armed soldiers in time of war. But however important a noble, if he caused trouble he could lose his lands, just like an ordinary villein.

This social system, which historians call *feudalism*, lasted in England and much of Europe throughout the Middle Ages. The beginning of the end of feudalism came with the *Black Death*. It killed so many people that landlords could only get serfs to farm the land by paying them wages, instead of taking rents from them. And, naturally, the serfs worked for whoever paid the most.

Sugar was almost unknown in the Middle Ages, and there were none of the cakes and sweets we have today. The only sweetener was honey. Each village kept some bees. In the summer it was important to catch the bees when they swarmed, otherwise the villagers would lose their honey.

England had many vineyards in the early Middle Ages, because wine was a popular drink. In the autumn the ripe grapes were picked and pressed into wine, either by foot or with a heavy wooden press. Monasteries often had vineyards and, in the picture, a monk is testing the new wine.

Medieval farm animals were much smaller than they are today. Most families kept a few pigs. In the autumn they were let loose in the woods to get fat on the nuts and acorns. Then they were killed and their meat smoked or salted to provide food for the family throughout the winter.

Villeins paying their rents. Details of the eggs, ducks, butter and vegetables each family paid were written down in the manor's account book by the bailiff. Cheating was severely punished. A cow's horn is fixed to the table, it holds ink for the *quill pen*.

Fierce wild animals roamed the countryside. Bears and wolves were quite common, especially in mountainous areas. Sheep flocks were protected by shepherds with huge dogs. These dogs wore spiked collars to protect their throats from the wolves' savage attacks.

Farming

Farming was the chief occupation for people all over England and Europe. Even villeins like blacksmiths and millers who did not work in the fields depended on it. The blacksmith made and mended tools and the miller ground the corn from the fields into flour.

The crops varied. Wheat and grapes were grown in the south of France, oats and rye in colder, wetter northern England and Germany.

Fields were divided into long thin strips, with no hedges or fences between them. The strips were narrow because oxen pulled the ploughs. It wasted time to turn these slow, clumsy animals around too often, so long thin fields were more practical than short wide ones. Oxen were lazy as well as slow. The length of the fields, 180m, was roughly the distance they would go before stopping for a rest. By 1400 many of the rich farmers were using horse-drawn ploughs, (horses were more expensive than oxen), but the tradition of long thin fields continued, as the picture shows.

Each family in the village had a number of strips in different parts of the farm. It was a nuisance getting from one strip to another, but it stopped one family getting all the good land and another all the bad. Not every family had the same number of strips. The most important had many more than the very poorest. But, rich or poor, everyone had to pay rent for their strips (p. 10).

Agriculture was very primitive by today's standards. The plough and harrow were the only machines used that a modern farmer would recognise. In spring, as the ground was ploughed, someone walked behind the ploughman carrying a basket of seed and scattering handfuls on the ground. Then came the harrow, pulled by oxen or horses to break up the soil and cover the seeds.

In good years families were able to grow enough for themselves with a little extra to sell. In bad years there was hardly enough for each family.

Corn from the fields was ground at the village mill. Mills were driven by wind or by water, as in the picture. The river turned the paddles of the mill-wheel. This forced the heavy mill-stones around, crushing the grain between them. A villein leads his donkey carrying a heavy sack of grain to the mill. His wife looks on. She is spinning wool into thread. Beside her is their baby, wrapped in *swaddling clothes*. In the reeds beside the mill-wheel lies a fish trap. Perhaps they are going to use it to catch fish or eels for their supper.

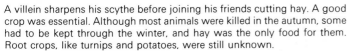

The wool trade was very important in medieval England, especially in East Anglia and, later in the period, the Cotswolds. As one wealthy wool merchant wrote in 1350: 'I thank God and ever shall. It was the sheep that paid for all.' Here men shear off the sheeps' woollen fleeces.

A villein sharpens his scythe before joining his friends cutting hay. A good crop was essential. Although most animals were killed in the autumn, some had to be kept through the winter, and hay was the only food for them. Root crops, like turnips and potatoes, were still unknown.

Villeins had little gardens around their cottages as well as their field strips. They did not pay rent for their gardens and could grow what they liked for themselves. One thirteenth-century writer described a garden growing peas, beans, leeks, parsley and shallots.

In the short days of the winter months little work could be done in the fields. But keeping warm was very important. Although the villeins' cottages were tiny, doors did not fit very well and windows were just holes in the wall. So collecting wood for fires and building repairs was essential.

Everyday Living

The two most important buildings in a village were the church and the manor house. Because of their importance they were usually built of brick or stone. The homes of the villeins were made of *wattle and daub*. The roofs were usually thatched with reeds or straw. These materials were very flimsy, which is why so few medieval village homes remain, although there are still plenty of churches standing.

The Church was an important influence on village life. The priest was the most important person in the village after the lord of the manor. Neither worked in the fields, the lord because he had villeins to do the work for him, the priest because the villeins had to give the Church a *tithe*, a tenth part of all their crops.

The Church was so powerful that it stopped people working on Sundays. It was a holy day so they had to go to church instead. The great Christian festivals of Easter, Christmas and Whitsun were also holy days and only essential work, like feeding and milking the cows, was allowed. The Church also celebrated special days as saints' days. These, too, were holy days and so days off work. And that is how we get our word 'holiday'! There are few holy days now, but the word 'holiday' is still used for a day off work.

Feasting and dancing were important parts of all village celebrations. The English were famous for their *caroles*. These combined both singing and dancing. Music was supplied by drums, pipes and a kind of bagpipe. Morris dancing, believed to have come from the *Moors* of southern Spain, became popular in the fourteenth century.

Some strict priests disapproved of dancing. In 1223 the Bishop of Salisbury stopped all dancing in churchyards. Although this sounds an odd place for a dance to us now, it shows just how closely the medieval church was involved with the community. But most people ignored the sermons that promised eternal damnation for too much dancing. Like Edward III (1327–77) who built a 'daunsyng [dancing] chambre' at Windsor for his Queen, people enjoyed the chance to feast and dance.

Although children were expected to help with their parents' work, there was still time for games. Many are ones we still play: spinning tops, bowling hoops, walking on stilts, riding hobby horses and playing with dolls. The children are playing with knucklebones made of real bone.

Rabbits were quite common in Europe, but were only introduced into England in the thirteenth century. Villeins hunted them with ferrets because they were good to eat and their skins were useful. Furry rabbitskin hoods and waistcoats helped keep out the winter cold.

During the long hard winters of northern Europe, villages near forests were often attacked by wolves. Traps of strong nets fastened to stout wooden posts were set to protect the villeins' animals. Wolf skins made nice warm rugs and cloaks.

A lame horse was no good to anyone, so horseshoes had to be carefully made. This was the job of the farrier. (The word comes from *ferrum*, the Latin word for iron.) He hammered the iron shoes into shape on his anvil, using tools very like those still used today.

Travelling from one village to another was difficult and dangerous. Roads were often just rough tracks and bands of robbers attacked wealthy travellers. At times of famine no-one travelled unless it was essential because there were so many robberies and murders.

Life in a Castle

Many castles were dotted across England and the countries of Europe. The richest and most important nobles lived in them. Castles were important in defending the kingdom against attack. They were strongly built, usually of stone, and had a commanding position over the surrounding country-side. Strong enough to withstand attack, castles were also used by rebel nobles as centres of resistance against their king. To stop this, no-one could build a castle without the king's permission. In England, during the troubled reign of Stephen (1135–54) many nobles built illegal castles. On the orders of the new king, Henry II, they all had to be pulled down or else given to him.

Castles were built for military purposes and were uncomfortable to live in. The thick walls made the living quarters cramped. Odiham castle in Hampshire had a tower 54 m round, but because the walls were 3 m thick the interior was only 11 m in diameter. The slit windows which stopped arrows being shot in, also stopped light and fresh air coming in.

The great hall was the castle's centre. There everyone met for meals, sitting on benches at long trestle tables. The lord and his family sat at a table on a platform at one end with any important guests. At night the tables were cleared away and the hall acted as a bedroom for most of the castle's servants.

Upstairs there was a small room called the *solar*. During the day it was the sitting-room for the lord and his family. At night it was their bedroom. Because it was smaller than the hall it was a bit warmer, but much of the heat from the great open fire went up the chimney. The windows were small, but they had no glass, just wooden shutters to keep out the draughts. There was little furniture: a few chairs and stools and a chest to hold valuables.

Although by today's standards it was very primitive, it was the only place in the castle where any privacy could be found.

Archers played such an important part in all medieval armies that in 1365 Englishmen were forbidden to play ball-games on Sundays. They had to practise archery instead. These men are using long-bows. There was also the cross-bow, but it was slower to shoot and was not popular in England.

Falconry, hunting game with birds of prey, was a popular sport among the rich. These two men are training a young falcon. The feathered hood is taken off and it flies to attack an imitation game bird. After weeks of training it will be taken out hunting and allowed to attack real prey.

In summer there was little time for leisure and in the winter there was almost no entertainment to while away the long dark evenings. A visit from some minstrels or *troubadours* was very welcome. These men travelled all over Europe, stopping for a few days at a castle or manor. In

return for food and lodging they entertained the lord, his family and his villeins with music, songs and stories. They told of the daring adventures of legendary knights and heroes. The Song of Roland, tales of the exploits of the knight Roland, and the story of King Arthur were always popular.

Bridge building increased during the Middle Ages. This made both travel and trade between different places much easier. But bridges were expensive to build and maintain. So everyone crossing a bridge had to pay a toll, a small sum of money, for using it.

Anyone who broke the rules of medieval society was swiftly punished. Perhaps this man had not paid his rent or had sold bad meat, so he must stand in the pillory for a day. The upper board is clamped around his neck and wrists and everyone else can jeer and throw things at him.

Travel and Trade

For many centuries after the sack of Rome in AD 410 and the collapse of the Roman Empire that followed, there was little peaceful contact between the states of Europe. Border raids were frequent and invasions common. But, as the centuries passed, times became more peaceful. A country that is not at war has time to develop trade and industry and so becomes richer. Medieval Europe slowly followed this pattern.

Roads were so bad that water was the safest and most reliable way of transporting goods. The great rivers of Europe, the Rhine and the Seine, the Elbe and the Danube, were busy thoroughfares alive with boats carrying goods across Europe.

Most trade by sea was handled by the Venetians in the south and the Hanse merchants in northern Europe. Venice, a small city state which centuries later joined with others to form modern Italy, had an excellent navy. Luxury goods from China and India reached Europe via Venice, through Turkey and the Middle East. Venice became enormously wealthy through this lucrative trade.

The Hanse merchants who controlled most of the sea-trade of northern Europe were based on the Baltic towns of Visby, Lubeck and Danzig. As they became rich and successful they built wharfs and warehouses in other ports, such as London and King's Lynn. They even minted their own money. And that is where 'sterling', the word for the British currency comes from – for these rich merchants were often called the Easterlings.

On land most goods were carried by pack-horses. Long trains loaded with bundles crossed the passes of the Alps between Italy, France and Germany, the same passes that the Romans had used for their invasions of Europe so many centuries earlier. But now instead of weapons the pack animals brought rich silks and spices from the East. Even more importantly, they brought the great culture and learning of the Arab scholars.

Marco Polo was the son of a Venetian merchant. In 1271 he set out with his father and uncle to buy silks and spices from the East. The Polos carried their merchandise on a long train of pack camels. When they reached the court of the khan, Marco was appointed adviser and stayed 17 years.

Merchants needed somewhere to spend the night and rest their horses, because it was unsafe to travel after dark. Inns grew up along the main trade routes. There were stables for the horses and a bench or rough straw mattress for the men. A typical inn is described in *The Canterbury Tales*.

Transporting fresh food was difficult. Canning and freezing were not invented until the nineteenth and twentieth centuries. In the Middle Ages the only way to keep food edible was to smoke, dry or salt it. Here fresh fish is being taken to a market. It has to be sold quickly, otherwise it went bad.

Merchants were often attacked and robbed. To travel alone was dangerous. One of the most famous of all robbers was Robin Hood. Perhaps he was only a legendary person, but England was covered with thick forests, like Sherwood Forest, where bands of outlaws and robbers could easily hide.

Apart from kings, nobles and merchants, no-one else travelled very much. There was no need. Families lived in the same villages for many generations, so there were no relatives elsewhere to visit. Anyway, the roads were so bad that travel was very uncomfortable. Rich men rode, but their wives and

daughters travelled in covered vehicles like this one. The wheels, like those of the cart, were wooden and studded with iron. The studs helped grip muddy surfaces, but made journeys over hard, rutted roads even bumpier, however many thick cushions the lady had to sit on in her carriage.

Markets and Traders

Medieval towns were busy and bustling, noisy and dirty. The narrow streets were full of people, animals and rubbish. Town councils tried hard to stop people dumping their rubbish in the street. Coventry council paid a dustman ½p a day in 1420 to take away rubbish. But it was no good, streets still remained full of smelly rubbish. To make matters worse, there were no drains or sewers, and only the streets in the centre of a town were paved. Think of the mud in wet weather and the smell all the year round!

The streets were so narrow and the houses so crammed together that people could shake hands across the street. The buildings were mostly made of wood or wattle and daub with tiled or thatched roofs. But this was very dangerous. Narrow streets of wooden houses burnt fast, and fire was a great hazard in medieval towns. London suffered serious fires in 1132, 1135 and 1161. Canterbury and Winchester also had disastrous fires in 1161. By law citizens were supposed to keep buckets for water and long hooked poles with which to pull off burning thatch, but fire was still a very serious problem. In London, by 1189, it was noticed that brick and stone buildings with tiled roofs did not burn so easily. A law was passed encouraging people to build houses of these materials. Unfortunately bricks and tiles were expensive, so only the rich could afford them.

The shops were tiny. Some in Oxford were only 2.5 m wide. Others, in Burford, Oxfordshire in the fifteenth century, were 5.3 m long, 2 m wide and 2 m high. Usually shops were the front room of the shopkeeper's house. Part of the front opened out into the street as the counter, another part opened upwards to provide some shelter if it rained. When business was over for the day the two parts closed together to form a strong shutter to keep out thieves.

Shopkeepers hung signs above their shops: a bowl for the barber, shears for the tailor, because most people could not read. With houses so low the signs could be quite dangerous for anyone riding along the street.

In small towns the few shops only sold ordinary, everyday things. So a peddlar's visit was always welcome. These men travelled from place to place all over Europe, selling little luxuries like braids and belts, mirrors and other fancy goods. They also brought news from the outside world.

The cloth trade was very important in medieval Europe. Much of the best cloth was woven in *Flanders*. Most of the buying and selling of cloth and wool took place at the big cloth fairs held in different European centres. The fair at St Denis on the outskirts of Paris was especially important.

As trade developed so did the use of money. Most villeins never saw any, but wealthy merchants began to use it more and more. The Italians gradually became the leading bankers and money-changers of Europe. This banker weighs out currency for a merchant to use abroad.

Another important trade was the spice trade. Venice was the chief centre for it. There the ships from the Middle East, laden with spices from India, Persia and even further east, unloaded their goods. The merchants and salesmen bargained noisily, sampling the spices and fixing the prices.

In the Middle Ages little was known about the causes of illness and disease, and even less was known about cures. Some were harmful and most were useless. Imagine a modern doctor prescribing the hearts of a robin and an owl to be tied round the head to cure insomnia! Perhaps this

apothecary's medicines were more effective. The Arabs of the Middle East and North Africa understood most about medicine at this time. As their contact with Europe increased, medical knowledge spread. Montpelier in France and Salerno in Italy both had important medical schools.

The Town in Danger

The Middle Ages were not peaceful times. Throughout the period there were wars and rebellions in every country. William I's conquest of Britain in 1066 was just another armed invasion of one kingdom by the ruler of another one. The tables were turned just over fifty years later when Henry I (1100–35) captured Normandy from his brother, Duke Robert.

A civil war, when different groups within one country fight each other, can be just as damaging as a foreign invasion. The Wars of the Roses, between the dukes of York and Lancaster and their followers lasted thirty years – 1455–85 and ended with the death of the Yorkist king Richard III at the battle of Bosworth Field. Although fighting did not take place everywhere, it still disrupted trade and agriculture over large areas of the country. This meant near starvation for many thousands of people and made the country very much poorer. Exactly the same thing had happened three centuries earlier during the reign of Stephen (1135–54) when Matilda, daughter of Henry I, tried to take the kingdom from her cousin.

Towns had to be well protected to withstand attack, whether by rebels or invaders. Strong high walls were very important. The gates into the town had heavy wooden doors reinforced with iron. Often there was a *portcullis* which could be lowered for extra protection. Walls had to be kept in good repair and, by the Statute of Winchester of 1285, Edward I ordered that the citizens should keep watch at the gates at night.

But sometimes walls were not strong enough to keep out the enemy. Then the inhabitants fled into the surrounding fields and woods. So many captured towns were sacked and the inhabitants put to the sword (killed) by invaders that it was better to flee than to stay and take a risk that the conqueror would not break his promise to be merciful to his captives.

Without radio, television or newspapers, news travelled slowly. If the king wanted people to hear something important quickly and accurately, he sent out heralds. These men went to the main towns, where buglers attracted people to the town's square. Then the proclamation was read to the crowd.

At night most towns had a curfew. Anyone found in the streets after dark was jailed for the night. This was really a security measure. As there was nothing to do in the unlit streets at night anyone caught there was bound to be a troublemaker. Or so the town councils thought.

The larger towns had special covered market halls. Here countrymen sold their produce, carefully watched by the market officials. These men fixed the price of the goods and checked the weights used by the stall-holders. Anyone who cheated by using false, light weights was fined.

Around the top of the town walls were walkways. Groups of townsmen took it in turn to patrol them, keeping a look-out for invaders or even armed robbers. If a guard saw anything suspicious he sounded his horn, the church bells were rung to warn people and the gates were quickly bolted.

Death was the punishment for murder, rebellion and even theft. A particularly unpleasant form was hanging, drawing and quartering. The prisoner was hanged, but before he was completely dead, his heart was cut out and his body cut in quarters.

The Cathedral Builders

Building the great European cathedrals was probably the greatest and most lasting achievement of medieval society. Just as wealthy merchants built churches to praise God, so kings, princes and bishops built cathedrals. From the eleventh century onward there was a great upsurge in building. The cathedrals of Durham and Canterbury in England and Bourges and Notre Dame in France were all started at this time. It is not surprising that they took years to complete. Imagine building something as tall as Salisbury cathedral without cranes, mechanical pulleys or even strong steel scaffolding.

Everything was done by hand. First the stone was quarried out of hillsides. Then it was taken to the building-site, often a great distance away. Transport was in slow, lumbering waggons pulled by teams of the strongest oxen. Sometimes the stone could be taken by water. This was quicker and easier, but it was still slow work loading and unloading the great pieces of stone.

When the waggons arrived the stone was unloaded and they returned to the quarry for another load. The craftsmen then started the slow job of cutting the blocks into the right shape. They used adzes, mallets and chisels – the only tools they had – to cut blocks several metres long and thick.

Once shaped, the stones were put in position. This was easy for the foundations and first few metres of the walls, but as the building rose it became ever harder. Scaffolding was made of wood lashed together with rope and *withy bands*. The workmen stood on rough planks or rush matting. The blocks of stone, and baskets full of the mortar to fix them, were hauled up by hand-wound pulleys. Sometimes the rope broke and the stone crashed to the ground below, smashing beyond repair.

The men who master-minded these projects were not architects as we know them but master-masons. They learnt their skills on the job. Of course there were some failures, but the great medieval cathedrals which stand today show just how well they learnt these skills.

These masons are shaping decorative blocks for the pillars of the cathedral. The man on the right traces out the shape with compasses. The other two cut the blocks into shape. In the background a team of oxen brings in another waggon laden with stone for the great building.

Every church and cathedral had the right to give sanctuary. Anyone – rebel, criminal or the wrongly accused – was completely safe if he reached the church and got hold of the handle on the wall or door. This caused many disputes between kings and bishops throughout the Middle Ages.

All medieval cathedrals were decorated with sculpture, especially around the great doors at the west end. The men who carved the statues were very highly skilled. They worked in sheds or *lodges*. The statues were usually religious but sometimes the sculptor carved the face of someone he knew.

Medieval churches and cathedrals were far more colourful than they are today. The walls were often painted with stories from the Bible. The many statues and the roof were also painted. Sermons were an important part of the church service and many fine medieval pulpits still survive.

One of the glories of the medieval cathedrals was the stained glass windows. They were the finishing touch in a building where 'everything soared towards God'. The cost was immense, for ordinary glass windows were so expensive that even the rich took their windows when they moved house.

Apprentices and Craftsmen

Throughout the Middle Ages all trades and crafts were strictly controlled by guilds. There was a guild for every type of business, for example, bakers, saddlers, goldsmiths, carpenters, masons, candlemakers and tailors among many others.

Each town's guilds were independent of those anywhere else, but they all made sure their members did good work. The guild's council sorted out complaints from the public, regulated prices and stopped unskilled workers giving the trade a bad name.

When a boy reached his teens he was apprenticed to a mastercraftsman. The apprenticeship lasted seven years and during that time the boy lived at his master's house. He got board and lodging and, if he was lucky, a little pocket money, but that was all. In fact, if a boy's parents were ambitious and wanted him to join one of the most important and powerful guilds, like the goldsmiths,

they had to pay the mastercraftsman. Apprentices were a good source of cheap labour for the craftsman, but without a craft it was difficult to get work, especially in towns, and being an apprentice was the only way to learn one.

The new apprentice did the simplest jobs, fetching, carrying and unloading the timber carts. Gradually he learnt the basic skills and was allowed to do other things. By the end of the seven years he was ready to pass the guild's test which was to make a fine piece of work – a coat, perhaps, if he was a tailor, or a splendid chest if he was a carpenter. If the piece was good enough he could call himself a mastercraftsman.

As a mastercraftsman the newly qualified apprentice could set up his own workshop and employ apprentices. But this needed money and experience. Most men worked for some years as *journeymen*, gaining experience and saving money until they could start a business of their own.

All dyes were made from natural materials such as bracken, moss and heather roots. These men are dyeing cloth. The plain cloth is pummelled around in a vat full of dye, heated by a fire underneath. Next the excess dye is allowed to drip away and then the cloth is hung out to dry.

A *reliquary* made of gold was a church's most precious possession. They were expensive to make for gold has always been costly, and craftsmen with sufficient skill to make such beautiful things were difficult to find. A reliquary like this took many months of hard work.

Watched by two guild officials, an apprentice silversmith works on his *masterpiece*. He is finishing off the decoration on a silver goblet. If it is good enough he will be able to call himself a mastercraftsman, because he made a masterpiece – and that is where our word comes from!

In the master-carpenter's workshop two churchmen examine a cupboard. It will probably be used in a church to keep the priests' robes. Meanwhile an apprentice marks out joints on a piece of wood. Mortice and tenon, dovetail and mitred joints were all used by medieval carpenters.

There were no ready-made clothes in the Middle Ages. People bought lengths of material and made the clothes themselves. If they were rich a tailor made the clothes for them. The men who sold the cloth were usually tailors, too. Tailoring was one of the few trades girls could learn.

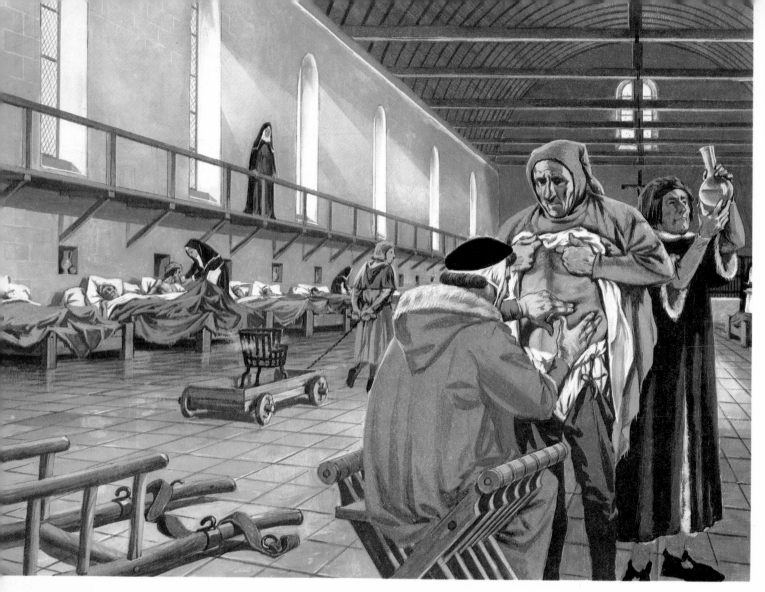

Sickness and Medicine

One reason for Europe's small population during the Middle Ages was the very high mortality rate. Many women died in childbirth and about one third of all children born died before they were five years of age. Anyone over 45 was considered really old. No-one understood the need for cleanliness and hygiene. Even if they had, it would have been difficult to practise, because drinking water came from open wells and the streets acted both as thoroughfares and sewers.

These conditions helped the spread of the plague. This disease was brought to Europe from the East by the fleas which live on rats. It reached England late in 1348. By 1351, when the worst was over, more than a million of England's 3½ million people had died. Outbreaks of plague continued throughout the Middle Ages, but were never again so severe.

There were few hospitals. One of the first in England was founded by Rahere, jester to Henry I, in 1123. Although rebuilt many times, his hospital is still there – it is St. Bartholomew's Hospital in London.

Montpelier in France and Salerno in Italy had famous medical schools (p. 21). However, because dissection was forbidden by the Church, it was difficult for anyone to learn how the human body worked. Not until men like Leonardo da Vinci in the fifteenth century had the courage to disobey the Church's rules did medical knowledge really make progress so that people were able to recover from minor ailments.

Poor diet did not help people keep healthy. Throughout the winter there was almost no fresh food. This was why spices were so important – they relieved the dullness of the dried, salted or smoked food. Lemons, oranges, grapefruit, bananas, tomatoes, potatoes and cauliflowers did not become part of people's diet for several centuries. Imagine a week's meals without them!

Leprosy was quite usual in medieval Europe, although many other skin diseases were probably also called leprosy. People suffering from the disease were forced to live as beggars. When they went through the streets they had to ring a bell or strike a clapper so people could avoid them.

Springs of mineral water were believed to be good for the health. Spas, where people swam and drank these health-giving waters, had been popular since Roman times. Bath in Somerset is a good example. There were also several in Germany and France.

Mothers had their babies at home. If they were poor a neighbour was just called in to help. The wives of rich men had nurses to help them and care for the new baby. Soon after birth, babies were wrapped in swaddling clothes. These were thought to give them strong, straight limbs.

The plague was a time of sorrow and anxiety. The rich fled from the cities, so spreading the disease further afield. At night the narrow city streets were full of funeral processions, as monks and priests collected the bodies of people who had died during the day.

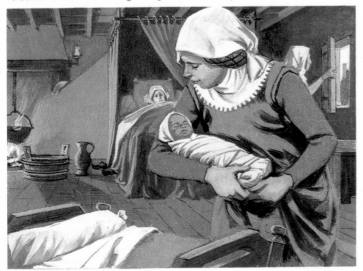

Dentistry was very primitive, although people probably had quite good teeth as they ate so little sugary food. The only sure cure for toothache was to remove the tooth. But there were no pain-killing injections, just a good drink of alcohol, a pair of pliers and someone to hold down the patient.

Feasts and Famine

Famine, war and plague were three great curses of the Middle Ages. Life was hard at the best of times, but when a hard winter followed a bad harvest starvation and famine were real possibilities (p. 12). Even in good years there was seldom more than just enough. Part of the problem was medieval agriculture (p. 12). No-one understood about fertilisers or breeding more productive crops, so yields stayed much the same. In fact, the threat of famine discouraged experiments. It was better to continue in the traditional way and produce something, than to risk changes, complete failure and starvation for the family.

Famine affected the poorest people most. The villeins with the fewest field strips and the smallest patches of garden were the first to suffer. With so little ground they could rarely grow more than a barely sufficient amount for themselves and their animals. If there was not enough food for the animals they had to be killed during the winter, which meant no milk or eggs and no calves or chicks in the spring. Replacement stock had to be bought, and they probably could not afford to do so. Relatives and neighbours helped, but a bad harvest affected everyone in a village.

Times of famine affected the rich, too. If there is nothing to buy, all the money in the world makes no difference. But plenty of money always makes life easier and the rich never suffered like the poor.

Food throughout the Middle Ages was monotonous by our standards, especially in winter. But on great occasions kings and princes enjoyed splendid feasts with many courses. Swans, venison, trout, pike and flounders were among the dishes guests ate at Henry V's coronation feast in 1413.

Table-manners were different from today's accepted standards. People ate with their fingers. They used knives to cut the really tough bits and threw the bones to the dogs. When Piers Gaveston, a friend of Edward II (1307–27), tried to introduce the use of forks, most English people thought that it was a nasty foreign habit.

The welfare state only began in this century. In medieval days beggars and the homeless were cared for by monks, nuns and some rich people. For example, Edward I paid for 666 poor people to have a meal every Sunday, but there was no properly organised help.

According to the rules of the Church in medieval times, no-one could eat meat on Fridays and the other fast days. However, fish was allowed, but it went bad so fast that only the abbeys, which had their own fish ponds, or people living near the sea or a river ever had it fresh.

Inns were busy places, especially on market days. The most popular drink on the continent was probably wine, while in Britain it was ale. The town councils decided prices and tested the ale for quality. If it was too expensive or not up to standard the innkeeper was fined.

In medieval towns and cities all shops of one kind were grouped together. Sometimes, even today, street names in the older parts of a city give us a clue about their past: Spicers Row, Pie Alley, the Shambles. Here our ancestors bought their spices, freshly made pies and their meat. The streets

Every town and village had a baker. The apprentice mixes the dough in a big wooden trough, while the baker takes the freshly made bread out of the oven. Some house-wives made their own dough, but it still had to be baked in the baker's oven, because no ordinary home had an oven.

where the butchers had their shops were usually called the Shambles. This was probably quite an appropriate name, because slaughtering was done on the spot, and there were always stray dogs and cats lurking around to grab at any scraps of bone and meat lying about.

Street Festivities

Town streets were always busy. Besides the everyday bustle there were other things to see: a nobleman and his followers in procession, a group of jugglers and acrobats, men with bears or monkeys dancing to the beat of drums or tambourines. The most popular of these entertainments were the mystery plays (p. 34). Although executions, usually in public to serve as a warning to others, were also very popular.

The grandest processions took place when a king was crowned or married. Then all the streets and houses were decorated. Rushes were scattered on the ground to cover the puddles and potholes. According to Matthew Paris, an English monk and historian, the crowds who came to watch the procession when Eleanor of Provence married Henry III of England in 1236 were so big 'that London, with its capacious bosom could scarcely contain them'. He also described how the citizens dressed in their best clothes. Those with horses had even bought 'glittering new bits and saddles'. The chief citizens 'carried with them 360 gold and silver cups' and in front rode 'the king's trumpeters with horns sounding'.

Not all processions were as cheerful and happy. At times of trouble solemn groups of monks walked through the streets chanting psalms and saying prayers. This was a public demonstration of repentance, because medieval people believed that troubles like plague and famine were God's punishment for men's wickedness.

Many of the street entertainers: the acrobats, the men with performing animals, travelled all over England and Europe. Stopping a few nights in each town, they gave their show and moved on. Not everyone approved of these people. Thomas de Chabham, writing in 1230, knew exactly what he thought: 'Some change and distort their bodies with shameful leaps and gestures or put on hideous masks. All such are damned unless they leave their trade.' He also criticised wandering musicians who played and sang at inns. They too, according to de Chabham, were eternally damned.

The most popular of all celebrations was the carnival. This marked the end of the long dreary winter months and the coming of spring. People looked forward to the longer, warmer days, to new crops and more food to eat after the dark, cold and probably hungry months. Everyone dressed up in costumes, disguising themselves as animals, jesters and anything else they liked. The most important person in the procession was the false bishop – a man dressed up as a bishop and riding on a donkey. The Church disapproved of the carnival, but wisely did not try to stop it.

All churches, however small, had a font. Here newly born babies were baptised. This was usually done within a day or two of the birth because the mortality rate was so high and medieval people believed that anyone who died unbaptised could not go to heaven.

Every church was dedicated to a special saint. Each year on that saint's holy day there was a procession. The priests walked through the streets carrying candles and other religious items, singing hymns and saying prayers. The people came to watch, often kneeling as the procession passed.

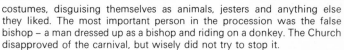

Trumpeters announce the arrival of the king. Most medieval rulers travelled around their kingdoms a great deal. People did not know what their ruler looked like unless they actually saw him. This made it very easy for imposters, like Perkin Warbeck, to pretend they were the real king.

It was a sign that times were bad to see a procession of flagellants. These monks walked through the streets, hooded and stripped from the waist up, chanting and whipping each other. In 1349 six hundred came to London during the Black Death. Twice a day they appeared in the streets.

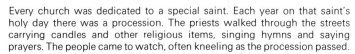

Art to Glorify God

The powerful medieval Church taught that serving God as a monk or priest was the greatest thing a man could do. But not everyone could be a monk or a priest. The next best thing was to serve God in one's work, glorifying heaven with art. Religious art also taught people about the Bible. Most people could not read, so they learnt about their religion from looking at pictures or watching plays.

The mystery or miracle plays were particularly popular. These had started as little plays to act out Bible stories in church. Gradually they became so popular that they took place in the churchyard. Slowly the plays changed, including comment on social topics and even criticism of the Church. This made the church authorities try to ban them, but the plays had become so popular that this was impossible. Instead the guilds took them over. Each guild chose a suitable story, the goldsmiths the adoration of the magi, the carpenters Noah's ark,

the wine sellers the marriage at Cana, and so on.

Members of the guilds performed the plays on big wooden platforms These were mounted on wheels and could be moved from one part of the town to another. Young men and boys played women's parts, as it was considered very immoral for a woman to act. Although scenery was limited, the guilds vied with each other to make the best stage effects. Hell's mouth, puffing flames and smoke, was always popular.

Plays varied from place to place, each town adding local comment. The plays of York and Chester still survive.

Probably the best known medieval play is Everyman. Its moral is that it is necessary to give up all worldly thoughts and material things in order to die happily and peacefully. People in the Middle Ages were very preoccupied with death because disease was so rife and people died so young.

Manuscript illumination was one of the greatest artistic achievements of medieval times. Monks painted miniature pictures and decorative patterns on the handwritten manuscripts. The colours, all made from natural substances, are as bright today as when they were painted.

Music was important in all medieval church services. Most of the larger churches and cathedrals had organs and choirs. The services at Salisbury cathedral were famous throughout England, but in 1322 the choirboys had to beg for their food as there was not enough money to keep them.

Carved pictures were another way of teaching people who could not read about the Bible and teachings of the Church. Bavaria, in southern Germany, has had a tradition of fine wood carving for centuries and Bible scenes carved by medieval craftsmen were exported to churches all over Europe.

Churches were very colourful in medieval times and church decoration was finest of all in Italy. Here artists are painting *frescoes* on the church's walls. To reach the high ceilings and domes of the church they worked on scaffolding. Giotto painted the frescoes in the Santa Cruce chapel, Florence.

Minstrels travelled all over Germany and other European countries, particularly southern France. They visited all the princes and nobles, entertaining them and their families with songs and poetry about the nobility of love and the service of God.

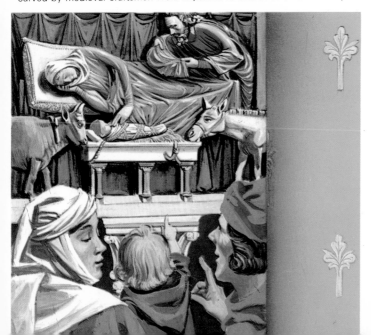

Education

Throughout medieval Europe education was in the hands of the Church. The teachers at schools and universities were all monks or priests. Usually only boys who were themselves going to be monks or priests went to school. Most girls never went, it was believed to be a waste to teach them reading and writing. Occasionally the daughter of a nobleman had lessons with her brothers and their tutor, but that was all.

There were three kinds of school: song schools, monastery schools and grammar schools. Then came university for those who were very clever or wanted to be doctors of theology, law or medicine.

At song schools the boys were taught to read and sing psalms and hymns, but little else. The village priest was the teacher, and no-one went unless he wanted to.

Monastery schools, as the name suggests, were part of a monastery. The boys at these schools usually became monks. They learnt to read and write, to do arithmetic and perhaps geometry. Lessons were in Latin because that was the language of educated people in medieval Europe.

Grammar schools were attached to a church or monastery, although by the end of the Middle Ages many were independent. The grammar taught was Latin grammar. One teacher called it 'the art of speaking and writing correctly, as do the writers of prose and poetry'.

The method of teaching was learning by heart. Because all books had to be written by hand (printing was not invented until the fifteenth century), there were few, so only the master had one. He read out a piece and the pupils had to repeat it after him and say it by heart. Discipline at all schools was very strict and beating was a common punishment.

Students at university were much younger than now. Seventeen was the usual age to begin studies, but many students went up at 13 or 14. Different universities specialised in different subjects. Paris was famous for theology and Bologna, in Italy, for law.

A geometry lesson. An English scholar, Adelard of Bath, wrote a text book on it during the reign of Henry I (1100–35). As there were no blackboards the master wrote on the stone floor with charcoal. Beside him is a stick, if a pupil cannot remember his lessons it will be used on him.

Each week students took it in turns to do special tasks. These included lighting the altar lamp, feeding the pet birds, sweeping the floors and making sure all the library books were in place. Many of the rarest and most precious books were chained to the library shelves.

Rich parents often paid for special teaching for their sons, to make sure they were ready for university. Or else they promised the monastery something special: a new altar, an expensive robe for the abbot, or perhaps a book for the library.

Students were often in trouble with the law, but sometimes the law went too far. Here, the head of the university makes sure that the town authorities will not be quite so harsh with his students again. This shows how powerful the head of a big university was.

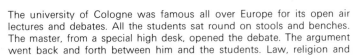

The university of Cologne was famous all over Europe for its open air lectures and debates. All the students sat round on stools and benches. The master, from a special high desk, opened the debate. The argument went back and forth between him and the students. Law, religion and philosophy were always popular subjects for debate. To get a Master of Arts degree, a student had to have a similar debate with his university teachers. This debate, or *disputation*, was to show off just how much he had learnt during his six years of study at university.

Soldiers of Christ

In the Middle Ages there was a great surge of reform in the monastic world. There had been orders of monks for many centuries – one of the earliest was started by Benedict of Nursia around AD 529. But the old strictness and religious ideals had almost disappeared in many monasteries and monks lived a very comfortable and in many cases an extremely dissipated existence.

In 1115 a French monk, Bernard, who was later made a saint, founded a monastery at Clairvaux in north-east France. He was a great reformer, bringing back the old idealistic ways and reviving interest in the monastic life. He also encouraged the second Crusade.

Christians in Europe regarded the Holy Land – the land around Jerusalem and other places mentioned in the Bible – as theirs because it was where Christ had lived and their religion started. In the seventh century AD the prophet Mohammed preached the Muslim faith in the Middle East.

Jerusalem and parts of the Christian Holy Land were also important to the Muslims, so conflict between the two was likely.

While Europe and the Christian Church were weak there was little trouble, but as kingdoms became more stable and the Church stronger, the chances of religious war increased. War between Christian and Muslim erupted in 1069 when the first Crusade (religious war) was preached by Peter the Hermit and blessed by Pope Urban II. The final Crusade, the eighth, was led by Louis IX of France in 1270.

Far from home, with inadequate supply lines, the Christians faced fierce warriors used to the hot climate. The Europeans were not. The knights were weighed down by their armour and the foot-soldiers were badly fed and exhausted from the journey. In military terms the Crusades were a failure, although they helped bring Europe into contact with a different culture and learning.

One of the best-known of all monastic orders is the Franciscans. The founder, St Francis of Assisi, was the son of a wealthy Italian family. He gave up his comfortable life and started the order in about 1209. Ever since, his writings have inspired people to follow his way of life.

The Cistercian monks get their name from the monastery founded at Cîteaux in Burgundy, south-east France, in 1098. It was intended to restore the old Benedictine order to its original discipline. The monks supported themselves, working hard on their farms and in their vineyards.

In the days before printing all books had to be written out by hand. This was a very slow process, especially as there was no artificial light and the work could only be done in daylight hours. The work was done by highly trained and skilful monks. They wrote on parchment, a material made from sheepskins. Although craftsmen were making paper in Spain in 1150, it was rare and expensive throughout the Middle Ages. The writing was done with ink and a quill pen. Any mistakes were scratched out with a small knife. The work was so detailed that many monks wore primitive glasses.

During the crusades two military religious orders were founded to fight in the Holy Land: the Knights Hospitallers and the Knights Templars. Both were very powerful. The Hospitallers made the castle of Krak des Chevaliers so strong that it withstood many long and fierce sieges.

It is midnight and the monks walk slowly and silently through the monastery cloisters to the chapel for the first service of the new day. All over the Christian world monks would be doing the same. No longer could they sleep through the night, the reforms of St Bernard and St Francis saw to that!

Pilgrims and Pilgrimages

Dotted all over Europe were shrines – important religious centres where people believed that a saint had performed a miracle. The Church taught that everyone should try to visit at least one shrine during his lifetime.

The best pilgrimage to make was, of course, to the Holy Land and Jerusalem. But the journey there was so long and difficult that only the very bravest went. Most people preferred to visit shrines in Europe. Rome, Canterbury and Compostella, in north-west Spain, were important centres of pilgrimage throughout the Middle Ages. But there were also smaller, local shrines. Walsingham in Norfolk was one of them. The Augustinian Priory founded there in 1061 was famous for its image of the Virgin.

Pilgrims travelled in groups for safety. Many went on foot, taking only a staff and a *scrip* with them. They lived by begging in the towns and villages they passed through, trying to imitate the poverty of Christ. According to one tenth-century book, pilgrims should not 'come into a warm bath, nor a soft bed and kiss no-one . . .'

Others preferred to travel in greater comfort. Many of the towns on pilgrimage routes became rich providing for these travellers' comforts. The group of pilgrims described by Chaucer in *The Canterbury Tales* certainly enjoyed themselves, riding slowly along each day, having a good meal and sleeping in an inn at night. Chaucer probably saw many groups on their way to and from Canterbury – there was even a guidebook for such travellers. The *Codex Callixtinus*, written in the twelfth century, gave information about roads, inns and shrines for the pilgrims to visit. But any pilgrim, rich or poor, had a difficult time if there was a boat journey: 'Men that sail to St James [Compostella] may say farewell to all pleasures, for many people suffer when they set sail . . . and they are likely to be groaning before midnight.'

All sorts of places were believed to have miraculous powers. At St Odile in Alsace, eastern France, a spring was thought to cure every kind of eye disease. Men and women travelled from far and wide to bathe their eyes in the healing water.

Some churches had miraculous relics which pilgrims visited. A relic could be the bones, clothes or anything else belonging to a saint. Many believed these cured disease. When Pope Boniface VIII organised the first holy year in 1300, thousands visited the tomb of St Peter in Rome.

Richer pilgrims stayed at inns, but poorer people could not afford to do this. All churches and monasteries on a pilgrimage route had to give shelter to pilgrims. Straw on the stone floor may seem uncomfortable to us, but most people slept on the floor in medieval times.

Pilgrims could buy all kinds of souvenirs when they reached the shrine at the end of their journey. Each shrine had a different symbol. The palm leaf showed that a pilgrim had visited the most holy of Christian shrines – Jerusalem. A scallop shell was the badge of St James of Compostella.

The Muslims controlled most of Spain beside the Middle East. Compostella, where St James' body was believed to have been found, was in the Christian part. As the pilgrims crossed the Pyrenees into Spain they planted crosses, the Christian symbol and that of the fight against the Muslims.

Heretics and Alchemists

Life was hard and uncertain in the Middle Ages. Because of this people feared and distrusted the unknown. Familiar things were safe, unknown or different ones dangerous. Anyone who questioned the king's laws was treated as a rebel and severely punished. Anyone who questioned or disagreed with the teaching of the Church was called a *heretic*.

Several heretical movements flourished in medieval times, for example the Lollards in England and the Cathars in France. Many of these movements wanted to return to a simpler form of Christianity. Peter Waldo, a French merchant who founded the Waldenses (*c.* 1175), preached an early kind of Protestantism. Like all heretics, however, he was cruelly treated and his ideas were not taken seriously for another three centuries. And it was another century before the Reformation, when Luther questioned the teaching and supremacy of the Church.

The Church's chief weapon against heretics was the Inquisition. This was founded around 1233 to suppress the Albigenses in southern France. Although the Inquisition was a Church court the priests who were the lawyers and judges often tortured their victims. The fate of anyone convicted as a heretic was hanging or burning.

Joan of Arc is probably the best-known person to have been burnt at the stake. To most ordinary French people she was a holy woman who had seen visions. To the English and French authorities her real crime was that she had dared to question existing beliefs, but for political reasons, the only way they could get rid of her was to condemn her as a witch.

Today we would probably call her eccentric, or a bit 'touched', but in medieval times only people who totally conformed were acceptable. No-one understood about mental illness or even physical deformities like squints or lameness. Anything that marked a person as different from the rest made him the object of suspicion. Even if not a heretic he might be a witch, and if convicted the sentence was the same – death.

Scientific knowledge as we understand it today did not exist, but that did not stop people experimenting and trying to discover the nature of things. The most popular experiment was how to turn ordinary metal into gold. Many men spent their lives trying to find out how to do this. Working away in secret laboratories, they risked being condemned as magicians and servants of the devil. Chaucer described them as smelling 'of brymstoon' (brimstone) and wearing 'threadbare array'. They were called alchemists, and that is how we get our word chemistry!

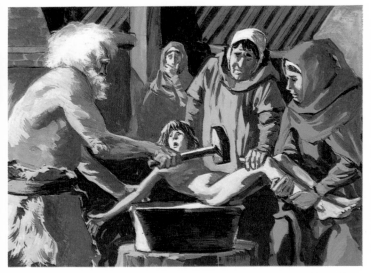

Folk medicine was widely practised because there was nothing else. Medical knowledge was limited (p. 28) and the few doctors stayed in the towns. Sometimes the village smith acted as the village healer, laying the sick child on his anvil and touching the aching part with his hammer.

Evil spirits were thought to come and live in the bodies of human beings. Anyone who suffered from fits or was slightly unbalanced was said to be 'possessed by the devil'. The church had a special service, exorcism, to try and drive out the spirits.

Anyone who suffered a sudden, unexplained illness or misfortune was believed to be the victim of witchcraft. Witches lived in caves or thick woods, making spells and boiling snakes, toads and fungi together in a cauldron to make magic potions. Or so people believed!

Before coal was mined on a large scale charcoal was used to heat smiths' forges. The men who made it, charcoal burners, lived lonely lives deep in forests, tending their covered fire-pits. Tales of strange woodland creatures were usually brief glimpses of charcoal burners at their work.

Kings and Princes, Noblemen and Knights

The office of king was sacred. Every medieval ruler believed that he was God's chosen ruler of his country. Even if he had won his crown by battle, defeating the previous king, as Henry IV defeated Richard II in 1399 and, a century later, Henry VII defeated Richard III, he still believed it was God's will. If it was not, he would not have won the battle. The coronation of a king underlined this belief. The crown was placed on his head by the country's chief churchmen, and it was they who gave him the orb and sceptre, the other symbols of his power. There is an echo of this medieval tradition in the English coronation service today, as it is still the Archbishop of Canterbury who actually places the crown on the head of the king or queen.

The beginnings of modern parliamentary government appeared in the Middle Ages. At first kings ruled with the help of a group of their most trusted noblemen. If a noble forgot his position and rebelled against his king there was trouble. But, if the king was weak, like King John (1199–1216), the nobles did as they liked and the country suffered. In England, during the reign of Edward I (1272–1307), the way of governing became more formal and better organised. The king appointed a council of noble advisers, often called the Great Council. Towards the end of his reign the word 'Parliament' was used for some of the most important meetings of this council. Then, as towns became more important, representatives from towns and counties were also summoned to the council meetings. Because these men were not rich noblemen, the king found them useful to reduce the power of the nobles, helping to curb their ambitions and keep them in check.

Parliamentary rule also developed in France under Philip IV (1285–1314). But in both countries the king was head of state and did not have to call council meetings unless he wanted to.

Because kings were appointed by God, it was believed that they had been given special powers. By touching a sick person the kings of France were said to be able to cure many illnesses. St Edward the Confessor, king of England 1042–66, cured a man who had been blind for nineteen years.

No king can run a country without money. This means taxing the people, collecting the money and keeping it safe. Just as each manor kept accounts, so the Court of the Exchequer kept the accounts of England. The money was stored in strong, iron-bound chests, deep in castle vaults.

Noblemen were given land by the king (p. 10). When a noble received his land he knelt and put his hands between the king's saying, 'I am your man'. Then the king gave him a coat-of-arms, banner and title. The Norman kings introduced this practice into England, to reward loyalty.

Trial by combat was often used to settle disputes. Based on the medieval belief that God helped the innocent, the accuser and the accused fought to the death. If the accused knight was killed people believed that he had been guilty. If he won it showed he was innocent after all.

The Pope was head of the Church. This led to many conflicts with rulers because the Pope appointed archbishops. These men were very powerful and acknowledged the Pope, not the king, as their overlord. Henry I and Henry II both had disputes with their archbishops, about this.

Tournaments and Jousting

Tournaments were probably the most popular of all medieval entertainments. Only knights could take part, but anyone could watch, if they managed to push to the front of the crowds. The few seats were reserved for the king, the queen and the most important nobles.

Tournaments had begun as mock battles, as a way of training knights and horses for real battle. Groups of knights and their men gathered at a specially chosen place. When the trumpets sounded the two groups charged at each other. Whichever group had the fewest killed, wounded or knocked off their horses won. Because these tournaments or *melées* were so rough and dangerous the popes tried to ban them between 1130 and 1316. The ban was ignored by Richard I (1189–99), who allowed five tournaments during his reign. In fact, in 1194 he legalised them to improve the fighting skill of the English knights, because the French were said to be better fighters than the English.

By the reign of Edward III (1327–77) tournaments had developed into jousting matches. These were much less rough and dangerous. Instead of groups of armed men charging each other, two knights, armed with long lances, galloped at each other, trying to knock the other off his horse first. By the end of the Middle Ages a barrier had been put between the two charging knights to stop them actually crashing into each other. Not everyone approved. One spectator grumbled that now they 'could only poke at each other'.

The knights often jousted for the honour of their favourite lady at court. If the lady consented she gave her knight a special favour, a brooch or scarf, to wear while he was jousting. Jousting societies were formed with special insignia and orders of chivalry and Edward III devised the Order of the Garter in imitation of King Arthur and his knights. A huge tournament was held to celebrate it.

Young noblemen underwent special training before becoming knights. As pages they learned good manners. Around the age of fifteen they became squires, riding, hunting and looking after the knights. Becoming a knight was a serious matter, and the night before the ceremony was spent in prayer.

The next day, after a special church service, the new knight was given his armour and *surcoat*. A squire buckled on his sword and handed him his shield and banner. Then he knelt before the king, who tapped him on the shoulder with his sword, saying 'Arise sir knight'.

Knights liked to prove themselves in battle. Those who returned in triumph from the crusades were specially favoured. Bathed in perfumed water and crowned with flowers, special feasts were given in their honour. Minstrels sang their praises, princesses admired them and kings gave them land.

Hunting was excellent training for fighting. Less dangerous, of course, it taught men to ride well and use weapons skilfully. Fierce wild boars lived in the dense forests that covered much of Europe in the Middle Ages. Hunting them was a very popular sport.

Life was lonely for the wives and daughters of knights away at war. Men fighting in the crusades were often absent for years. The only way of getting to the Holy Land was in sailing boats from Italy or else over land. Minstrels and troubadours provided entertainment for those at home.

War!

European rulers united in campaigns against the Muslims in the Holy Land, but more frequently they fought each other. Almost throughout the Middle Ages, England and France were at war. It started in 1066, when William, Duke of Normandy, invaded England claiming that the English crown had been promised to him by Edward the Confessor. He defeated Harold and successfully ruled England until his death in 1087. Later his son, Henry I, captured land in Normandy. And so it continued. For several centuries the English king had a much larger kingdom in France than in England. As late as 1474 Edward IV raised taxes to pay for another campaign in France. However he and the French king, Louis XI, came to terms. There was no war, but the English people did not get their tax money back either.

England was not part of a United Kingdom as it is today. Wales had been a separate country until subdued by Edward I, who made his eldest son the first Prince of Wales. It was to confirm his control of Wales that Edward built the great castles of Conway, Beaumaris and Harlech among others. Ireland and Scotland remained separate kingdoms throughout the Middle Ages. One of the fiercest medieval battles between Scots and English was the Battle of the Standard in 1138.

Not all battles were fought in the open like this one. Siege warfare became a highly developed art. Many medieval castles were so strongly built that there were no weapons strong enough to knock down the walls. Then an attacking army's best weapon was patience. The commander made his men camp all round the walls, so no-one could get in or out. If the siege lasted long enough the people starved. During the siege of Rouen (1418–19) cats and dogs were killed for food because there was nothing else. Before the city finally had to surrender, the brave citizens even ate rats and worms.

'Scorched earth' was another weapon used by both attacking and defending armies. Crops were burnt and villages destroyed so that an army with weak supply lines had great difficulty feeding itself.

At times of war knights had to provide their lords with armed men. The number each knight supplied depended on the size of his estates. He called up his villeins for service. They had no armour or weapons of their own, so the lord had to provide all their equipment.

The English army loads its fleet before leaving for a campaign on the continent. When Edward III marched to Paris in 1360 he had 'six thousand carts, each with four good cart-horses brought out from England' Imagine getting them across the Channel in the little boats of the time.

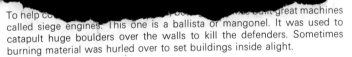

To help co... ...Built great machines called siege engines. This one is a ballista or mangonel. It was used to catapult huge boulders over the walls to kill the defenders. Sometimes burning material was hurled over to set buildings inside alight.

The Holy Land was not the only place where Christians and Muslims fought each other. During the Middle Ages most of the countries we now know as Spain and Portugal were occupied by the Moors. These fierce Muslim warriors from North Africa dominated the area from the eighth

century until finally driven out at the end of the fifteenth century. During the many long sieges of the strong Moorish castles, the noblemen and knights made themselves comfortable with large, well-furnished tents. But, as usual, life was tougher for the ordinary foot soldiers.

The Thick of Battle

Most campaigns were fought in the spring and summer. The better weather made marching easier. The baggage waggons, cannon and siege engines did not get stuck so often in the muddy tracks and badly made roads. Early in the Middle Ages most of the foot soldiers were villeins drafted into the army (p. 10). They disliked fighting because it meant leaving their fields and growing crops – anyone who could dodge service did. Things got worse in England after the Black Death of 1348–49. Gradually nobles began to hire *mercenaries*. In return for food, a small wage and the promise of as much loot as they could carry these men stayed for a whole campaign.

Medieval armies seem quite small to us, probably consisting of less than 20,000 men. But this is not surprising as the population of the whole of Europe was smaller than that of the British Isles today. In fact, proportionately, these armies were about the same size as those of late nineteenth-century Europe!

Archers were the great strength of the English army and were much feared by enemy forces. An eyewitness at the Battle of Crécy (1346) where the English were outnumbered three to one, described the English arrows as falling as thick as snow.

The gay banners carried into battle and the coats of arms worn by the soldiers served a very practical purpose. It was impossible to recognise someone wearing a helmet with the *vizor* down, so badges were used to identify friend from foe.

Medieval armour was heavy and cumbersome. Knights had to be helped on to their horses and if they fell off in battle, or the horse was killed under them, they had no chance of escape. Fortunately for them, knights were rich men so they were captured rather than killed. After the battle was over each side held its captives to *ransom*. Foot soldiers usually wore a mail shirt, leather jerkin and helmet. They were not ransomed.

Miners at work trying to remove the base of a castle wall so that it collapses. A wooden shelter protects them from the weapons hurled down. When the Black Prince besieged Limoges in France in 1370, miners successfully undermined the walls so the English troops could enter the city.

Once a city was taken the defeated townspeople received little mercy. Soldiers killed, looted and burnt. Their commanders did not try to stop them. On long campaigns money to pay the troops soon ran out, and often it was only the promise of loot that kept the army together.

Cross-bows (picture top right) were introduced into Europe around 1100, but the English preferred long-bows as they were quicker to fire. The best arrowheads were made of Sheffield steel. Cross-bows were so dangerous that popes tried to ban them – except for fighting the Muslims!

Climbing the walls was one way of getting into a city or castle. It was not usually very effective, as the men climbing the ladders were easy targets for the defenders' spears and arrows. Sometimes it was a useful way of distracting the defenders if the real attack was coming elsewhere.

A knight honoured on the battlefield for his bravery. This was a popular part of medieval stories, but it was based on fact. Edward the Black Prince, eldest son of Edward III, received his knighthood on the field of Crécy in 1346, after his outstanding part in the English victory.

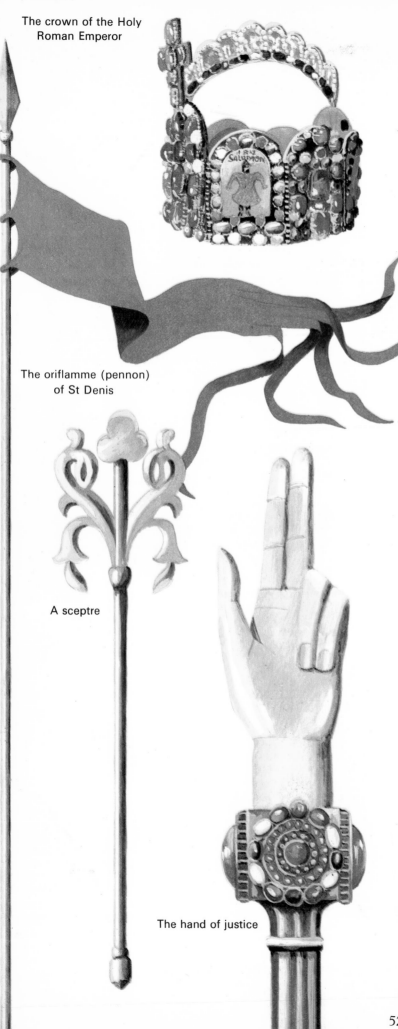

The crown of the Holy Roman Emperor

The oriflamme (pennon) of St Denis

A sceptre

The hand of justice

Coats of Arms

His coat of arms was a medieval knight's identity card. In a society where very few people can read, any form of badge or emblem is very important. The shields and banners carried by medieval knights were not just decoration, nor were they just a means of telling friend from foe on the battle field, although this was an important part of their purpose. In a highly decorative but nonetheless very specific way, anyone could tell by looking at a coat of arms who the knight was, what family he came from and the background of that family.

Servants of noblemen wore their lord's badge, so, at a glance, everyone knew who a foot soldier or manservant served. The lord's personal standard, with his coat of arms flew from the battlements of his castles and any stranger to the area could tell at once who the local lord was and what family he came from.

The design of a coat of arms was and still is very formal. Two emblems side by side on one shield are described as impaled. Four small ones on one shield (2 opposite) are said to be quartered. In the language of heraldry red is called *gules*, yellow is *or* and blue is *azure*. When an animal appears on a shield it can be *rampant* (7 opposite) or *couchant* (2 opposite).

Coats of arms were not restricted to kings and noblemen. Towns, universities, cathedral dioceses also had them. Towns usually bought the right to a coat of arms. In return for paying the king a large sum of money, a town received a charter, a large degree of independence from the local nobleman and the right to hold a market. This last was very important because it was a good way for a town to make money. Selling charters was also a good way for kings to raise money. Richard I and John sold charters to over 250 towns.

The monarchies of Europe all had their coats of arms and special emblems. The sceptre was one. The sceptre of the English kings was a richly jewelled golden staff mounted with a cross.

The kings of France also had the title of Chief Justice, and their sceptre showed the hand of justice.

When the French king rode into battle, the red oriflamme or pennon of St Denis was carried in front of him. The English king's personal standard was a red banner with golden lions rampant.

1 2 3 4 5

Some of the coats of arms worn by noblemen and their followers in battles or tournaments. The arms of Henry IV of England (2) and the Percy family (1) and those of the knights of Coucy (3) and Montmorency (4).

6 7 8 9 10

Some examples of arms belonging to towns and cantons: the badges of Pérouse (5), Barcelona (6), those belonging to the Guelphs of Florence (7), the badges of the province of the Tyrol (8), of Navarre (9) and of the canton of Uri (10).

The scallop shell, the badge of pilgrims who had been to Compostella

At tournaments and jousts, knights often wore favours given to them by the ladies of the court in whose honour the knights were fighting

The badges of the weavers and millers; all guilds had emblems showing the tools of their trade or their patron saint

The cross of Malta, badge of the Knights Hospitallers of the order of St John of Jerusalem

The five-cross symbol of the military order of St Sepulchre

Towns with a charter chose emblems to affix to their official documents

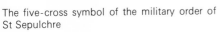

A knight

Villeins

A merchant

A lord and
his lady

Noblewomen

Fashions and clothes

Interest in fashion and clothes is nothing new. Although fashions changed much more slowly in the medieval period than they do today, they certainly changed. For example, in the early years of the period, around 1100, noblewomen wore on their heads a simple, fine linen covering, kept in place by a pretty bandeau. But by the end of the period, in the fifteenth century, womens' headdresses had become very elaborate. The fashion then was for tall, pointed cones made from splendid materials and hung with filmy and embroidered materials.

The materials from which clothes were made were, of course, very different from what we know today. There were no artificial, man-made fibres, everything was made from natural things: wool, linen (from the flax plant) and silk.

Most of the clothes would also seem very drab in comparison to ours. There were none of the bright, chemical-based dyes we can use. Dyes were all made from natural substances (p. 35). People used what was most easy to obtain, bracken, tree bark, heather roots and so on. Most of these produce rather soft colours. The brilliant reds and blues worn by the kings and princes were coloured with much rarer, and therefore more expensive, dyes.

There were strict laws regulating the kinds of clothes people could wear. These were called sumptuary laws. In 1363, Edward III decreed that: 'al manner of people that hath not 40s[1] of goods nor of cattals shal not take nor weare no maner of clothe but blanket and russet wolle of 12d[2] . . .' Anyone caught wearing more expensive clothing had to forfeit it to the king.

Fashions had their critics in medieval times, too. In his *History of England*, William of Malmesbury complained that at the court of William II (1087–1100) discipline had broken down because of the elaborate fashions all the courtiers wore. 'Then was there flowing hair and extravagant dress; and shoes curved with points; then the model of young men was to rival women in appearance.' Written in 1125, this still sounds very familiar!

[1] 's' stands for shilling. There were twenty shillings in a pound sterling.

[2] 'd' stands for denarius, a Roman coin of varying intrinsic valuè; 'd' was used as the abbreviation for a penny. There were twelve pennies in a shilling, 240 pennies in a pound.

Various styles of head covering worn during the Middle Ages. Made of wool and cloth, or fur for the rich, they protected the head against the cold and the wet.

Soldiers needed greater protection for their heads. For them there were hoods of chain mail and close-fitting metal skull caps. For those who did not fight the long woollen hood could be worn in different ways.

Breeches worn by villeins in the Middle Ages. Usually knee-length, they could be hitched up or lengthened according to the work the villein was doing. Coats of mail protected the knight. His wife kept the castle keys when he was away.

Noblewomen wore cloaks, or mantles, fastened at the shoulders with a cord. There were many different styles of shoe and boot. The three on the left were worn by villeins, while those on the right were worn by fashionable noblemen at court.

Tales of Medieval Animals

Constantinople 1204
Entering the city by the Charsais gate, the Crusaders of Lombardy saw in front of them lions and leopards, wandering around unchained. The animals attacked the soldiers fiercely, growling and clawing at them like demons. The soldiers fought back, using their spears, lances and swords. They killed the lions quite quickly, but the leopards fled, leaping on to the ramparts of the city's walls and the rooves of the houses.

Switzerland 1225
William d'Ecublens, bishop of Lausanne, angry at the way in which eels were infesting Lake Geneva, condemned them to be restricted to only one part of the lake.

At Croire, in the canton of Grisons, the judges at a local court upset at the way in which cockchafer larvae were attacking all the plants, summoned the larvae to appear before them in court.

Because the larvae were also part of God's creation, the judges decided not to have them killed. Instead they sentenced them to be banished to a remote and isolated area where it did not matter what harm they did.

Rome 1235
In a papal bull published to condemn their heresies, Pope Gregory IX formally accused the heretic Cathars of the crime of worshipping black cats.

France 1245
The Council of Lyons deposed the Holy Roman Emperor and King of Sicily, Frederick II, describing him as a sea monster, with claws of a bear, who 'enraged like a lion, can only utter insults and blasphemies against God.' Pope Gregory IX had already excommunicated Frederick in 1239. But Frederick took no notice. In Palermo, Sicily, he opened a zoo, collecting wild animals from all over Africa and Asia. He studied them closely and even wrote a book about them.

London 1251
Henry III, King of England, received a gift of a white bear and he made the City of London pay for its keep. It was quite usual for the bear and its keeper to be seen fishing on the banks of the Thames. It seemed as if the bear preferred fish to the meagre food provided under duress, by the Aldermen of the City of London!

Paris 1254
The French king, Louis IX, called St Louis, sent an elephant, which he had brought back from the Holy Land, to his brother-in-law, Henry III, the King of England. The Aldermen were so impressed, they built a special elephant house for him in the City of London.

Strange and Wonderful Tales from Travellers 1254
When the Flemish William of Rubreuck was received at the court of Mangu Khan, nephew of Ogoday Khan, third son of the mighty Genghis Khan, he saw an extraordinary fountain which was made of silver and shaped like a tree supported by four lions. Four different drinks spouted from the four lion heads: wine, koumis, mead and rice beer. Even more amazing is the story told by the Venetian Marco Polo who spent sixteen years in the service of Kublai Khan, another grandson of Genghis Khan: 'On the sacred day of spring,

the ninth of May in our calendar, the khan's courtiers assembled 10,000 stallions and mares of an immaculate whiteness. These horses were considered sacred and could graze anywhere on the khan's lands without fear. Only the khan and his family could drink the mares' milk as an offering to the gods.'

In the same book, Marco Polo tells us another story: 'The Khan of Tartary liked hunting, and he kept in the town of Cambalou, a great number of lynxes, leopards and eagles for this purpose. He also had a considerable number of lions, larger than those of Babylon, with beautiful striped coats of black, white and red. He used these strange beasts to hunt boars, bulls, wild donkeys, bears, stags, harts and many other animals. The lions travelled in cages, mounted on wagons, each with a little dog to keep them company. (These 'lions' were probably tigers. It is recorded that some of the eastern princes knew how to train them.)

Ethiopia 1257
The King of Ethiopia sent a giraffe to the Emperor of Constantinople, which was paraded through the streets for the enjoyment of the people.

Florence 1273
(From the Florentine chronicles of Giovanni Villani)
A very fine, but fierce lion was given to the city. It was kept in the menagerie in the square of San Giovanni. One day, its keeper forgot to shut the lion's cage properly and the lion escaped, running through the streets and jumping over garden walls terrifying the people. It pounced on a small boy in the garden of San Michele and seized him in its powerful jaws. But just as it was about to run off, the small boy's mother rushed at the lion and tore her child from it. At the same time, men with nets arrived and they recaptured the lion and led it back to its cage.

Portugal 1294
That well-loved king of Portugal, Denis (whom his loyal subjects called The Liberal) loved hunting. One day he was hunting in the mountains around Béja when he found himself confronted by a huge bear which leapt on him and brought him and his horse to the ground. The noble prince attacked the beast single-handed and

slew him with his dagger. In memory of this incident, the king had a live bear captured by his men, and ordered it to be taken to his palace of Fuellas for the amusement of the ladies and gentlemen of his court.

Clairvaulx 1300
The monks of the Abbey of St Bernard were given several beasts called Indian buffalo. Their meat and milk was thought to be as good as the meat and milk of cows and bulls and worthy of a nobleman's table.

Duchy of Poitou 1300
An Irish sailor, called Patrick Walltom, was the sole survivor of a terrible storm which drove his ship onto the rocks of the Bay of Aiguillon. He told how he discovered that it was possible to cultivate shellfish called mussels which were very good to eat. Having tried to snare sea-birds, with the help of nets staked out just under the surface of the water, he noticed how the nets became encrusted with mussels. This man created mussel beds by sinking hundreds of stones in the sea, which gave him a large crop.

England 1305
The peasants managed to dodge the royal decrees on hunting which forbade them to use dogs when hunting deer and wild boars. The woodmen of the New Forest found a way of training pigs to drive game out into the open, but no one knew by what devilish means they succeeded in gaining their dishonest ends.

Chateau-Landon 1323
(From the Chronicle of St Denis)
The local townspeople heard distressed cries which proved to come from a cat buried deep underground. They dug into the spot where they heard the cries and found a cat shut in a casket with plenty of food. The provost unmasked the guilty ones who had performed this magic rite: An Abbé of Citeaux and several of his monks. Under torture, they admitted that they were in contact with the Devil. Two of the men were banished and two others were burnt at the stake.

Rome 1328
Just as he was about to enter the city, King Louis IV of Bavaria ordered all the bells of the churches to ring out in his honour. As a result of this, the Pope excommunicated him for his pride. A monk who had stood out against the King's fantasy was tied to the end of a wooden beam, on the King's orders, and lowered into the ditch where the lions were kept. Torn to pieces by the beasts, he was then fed to the lions of the Capitol.

France 1350
By order of King John II, called The Good: 'No person may be so bold as to have, keep, feed, or maintain pigs within the walls of the city of Paris, and those persons who are found to disobey this ordinance will be fined ten sous. Furthermore, the pigs will be slaughtered by the city officials, or anyone else who finds them, and their carcases will become the property of the said city.'

The evils of the Tarantella

The Italians gave the name of a fever to this abominable dance, which every year, on the advent of summer, infected those who took part, with the madness of wild beasts. This abandoned dance was finally conquered at Metz in Lorraine by a pious knight who was visiting the city. One night he was sitting in his lodging, pondering how to save these poor, tormented people, when he noticed a black cat crouched in his fireplace staring at him fixedly. The noble knight made the sign of the cross, and this creature of the Devil disappeared, but not before it had uttered the most awful blasphemies. The townspeople, thanks to the grace of our loving Saviour, Jesus Christ, were found to be cured of the demonic power which forced them to dance.

To make sure that cats would never again tempt the citizens of Metz with this evil dance, it was decided to commemorate this miracle, on the 23rd June every year, by burning thirteen cats at the stake to thank the Lord and obtain his grace. The Aldermen of the city and the halberdiers marched round the stake three times, then the Mayor and the Governor, carrying lighted candles, lit the fire.

Paris 1333

King Philippe VI of France set up his menagerie of lions and leopards in a barn situated on the corner of the rue Fromenteau and the rue de Beauvais.

A chronicle of the noble art of falconry

It is advisable to remind everyone that priests and ecclesiastics will no longer have the right to place the falcon on the north side, the Gospel side, of the altar of our Lord God: a practice condemned time and again in the past.

A new and recent edict of King Charles VI of France forbids the common people to take hawks from their nest or to raise them for their own use. All confiscated birds must be brought to the Lord of the Manor who will see that they are kept and put to the service of the king's courtiers.

Edward III, King of England, has ordained that those found guilty of the theft of a falcon will be punished by death. He has also ordained that those found guilty of taking a falcon's nest

should be imprisoned for a year and a day. The king regards his hawks with the highest esteem and recalls that his noble father, Richard I of England, surnamed 'The Lionheart', having lost one of his birds at the siege of Acre in the Holy Land, paid one thousand pieces of gold to the Saracens as a ransom for it.

Falconry is highly esteemed in the East, so much so that Marco Polo tells us that he saw huge numbers of falconers in Asia. The Great Khan of Tartary appointed a court official to guard against any abuses which could result in the loss of falcons.

It was the duty of this official to keep any hawks which were brought to him until their rightful owners could be found. Kublai Khan kept more than two hundred gerfalcons in his summer palace. When he hunted, mounted on

an elephant, he kept the twelve best birds at his side, and was accompanied by ten thousand men with whistles who formed a vast circle to retrieve the hawks. At the court of this mighty emperor, each bird had a silver plaque attached to its claw, with the name of its owner, and that of its falconer, engraved on it.

The Duchy of Burgundy 1363
The funeral of Philip of Rouvres, twelfth duke of Burgundy, took place at the Abbey of Citeaux. A page led the duke's horse to the altar so that it could take part in the ceremony.

Switzerland 1374
The judges of the city of Basle found a cock guilty of a crime against nature and condemned it to death. It was accused of having laid an egg which was placed by its side at the stake, set up at the highest point of the Kuhlenberg hill.

Paris 1375
King Charles V of France, called 'The Wise', moved the menagerie of the late king Philip VI from the house of the king's lions in the rue Fromenteau to his palace of Saint-Pol which had been completed. The guardianship of the lions was entrusted to Guy Martin who succeeded his father to the post of Keeper of the King's Wild Beasts.

Vaucluse 1381
It was forbidden to take a swarm of bees from less than one hundred paces from its hive, or a swarm which belonged to others, under pain of a fine of five sous and the return of the bees.

Advice on the proper use of horses
Those who are unacquainted with the writings of Geoffrey of Preuilly, who listed the rules of the tournament, have the habit, in the choice of their mounts, of employing terms which bear no relation to their correct use. The charger, which is the horse of the knight, owes its name to the fact that it is always led onto the tournament field by a page holding it on the right. The palfry is a smaller, more lively horse which is only ridden for hunting boars, wolves, bears and stags. The hack is a mount most suited to women. The cob should only be used on

journeys, because it can bear the weight of luggage. Work-horses should be employed according to their owners' needs: pulling the plough or dragging loads of wood or stones.

Certain food which was authorised by the Church to be eaten during Lent because it was considered to be fish, not meat
The following food, in the guise of fish, was authorised for consumption during Lent: the flesh of new-born rabbits which had never left their warren, and the foetus of unborn wild rabbits.

It was forbidden by order of King John of France, called 'The Good', to enlarge existing warrens, or to establish new ones because the harvest had to be protected. Since 1287, the Bishop of Mende, William Durand, had also allowed hares to be eaten during Lent. The monks of Villeneuve-en-Avignon were famous for the way they prepared hare in a sort of sausage which had a very similar taste to sausage prepared from pork.

Wild Animals in Medieval Europe

Europe had many more different types of wild animals during the Middle Ages than it has today. The large areas of uninhabited woodlands and forests and the huge tracts of uncultivated heath and moorland provided good shelter for animals. The small human population meant that animals and men were not competing in the same regions for places to live. There was still room for both to live in harmony.

In the forests lived deer. Red deer, fallow deer and roe deer were the three main European species. Reindeer lived in large herds in Scandinavia and the very north of Europe. All these animals were good to eat. Hunting all deer, except the reindeer, was the sport and privilege of kings. Special forests were created in which the deer could live undisturbed by anyone except royal hunting parties. The New Forest is an example of such a forest. When William Rufus (King William II) was killed in a hunting accident there in August 1100, people said that it was a just punishment for the cruelty he and his father, William the Conqueror, had shown to people in the area. Many had had their homes destroyed when the forest was created and anyone caught poaching was punished very severely.

Wolves were quite common in Europe, although less so in England. They were particularly dangerous in winter. Villages on the edge of forests frequently had their flocks and cattle attacked. But, when hungry, the wolf is as cunning a hunter as the fox, and it was very difficult to protect livestock from these attacks.

Bears were also quite common, especially in mountain areas. According to Gaston de Foix, writing *c.* 1390, bears only attacked man or his animals if wounded. Otherwise they lead peaceful lives, relying on their sharp sense of smell to warn them of danger. Dancing bears were always popular as street entertainment (p. 32). These bears had probably been caught as cubs after their mother had been killed by hunters. Then they were hand-reared and taught to do simple tricks by their owners.

Beavers lived in many European rivers, from Kiev to Andalusia. They were hunted for their fur. The glands of the male produced a kind of musk which was used in the preparation of cosmetics and ointments which were sold by the travelling peddlars.

Another very rare animal was the auroch. This was the European cousin of the North American bison – which, of course, no-one knew about in the Middle Ages. Large and rather slow-moving, the auroch lived in the region of the Vosges and the great forests of central Europe, unlike the American species which lived on the open prairies.

Wild boars provided good sport for daring huntsmen. If cornered or injured a boar will turn on its attacker, fighting fiercely for its life. Many a hound was killed or badly injured by a boar's sharp tusks.

The ibex, with its long curved horns, was quite a common sight in the Pyrenees. The people of the region used ibex skins to make shoes that were both warm and and water-proof. The meat made good winter eating. But the ibex was a difficult animal to hunt, a few leaps up the mountainside soon took him out of reach of the hunter's arrow or his hounds.

A description of the Isle of Ely in about 1090 shows just how much wild-life there was. According to a French knight who knew the Isle, there was 'a multitude of wild animals: stags, roes, goats and hares found in its groves and by these fens. Moreover there is a sufficiency of otters, weasels and polecats. . . . In the eddies at the sluices of the meres are netted eels, large water-wolves, pike, burbot, and roach. . . . As for the birds . . . there you find geese, teal, coots, dabchicks, water-crows, herons and ducks, more than one man can number. . . .'

Medieval Books about Animals

Medieval people were just as interested in animals as we are today. Books were very rare, as everything had to be written out by hand (printing was not invented until the end of the fifteenth century). But even so there were quite a number of manuscripts about animals. Of those that have survived, perhaps the most famous is *The Story of Renard*. The fox, Renard, is the central character, and all the other characters in the story are animals. It is not, however, a work about natural history. It is really a satire on the contemporary feudal society.

Hunting and hawking, because they were such popular sports, inspired many authors. In studying the habits of the birds and animals that they hunted, men learnt quite a lot about natural history. One of the finest of these manuscripts is *The Book of King Modus and Queen Ratio*, written in 1379 by Henry of Ferrières. Chapters in his work cover subjects such as: capturing wild animals, snaring birds and training hawks and hounds.

But the most interesting of all the manuscripts is *The Book of the Hunt*, written by Gaston, count of Foix and viscount of Bearn. A man who wrote poetry and enjoyed the arts, Gaston was nevertheless a skilled and, in fact, quite brutal huntsman. In his book he describes the delights of the chase and the ways of catching the various animals that lived in the woods and forests of medieval France.

Poor Frederick II, King of Sicily, was thought mad by some and a dangerous heretic by others. But his book about falconry shows his interest in birds. Indeed, many of his observations about them and the way they lived were so ahead of his time that people thought it a further sign of his madness. Only centuries later, when knowledge of ornithology had increased, did people realise that he was right after all.

New Words

Apothecary Medieval chemist who made his own medicines

Bailiff Man in charge of a nobleman's estate

Black Death Bubonic plague which killed many thousands of people in England and Europe

Carole An English country dance combining both singing and dancing

Disputation Learned argument between university students and teachers

Feudalism Term used to describe the social and economic structure of medieval society

Flanders Area of Europe approximately modern Belgium, southern Holland and northern France

Fresco Picture painted directly on to a wall or ceiling before the plaster has dried

Guild Association of craftsmen or merchants in the same craft or trade

Heretic Someone who follows religious teaching banned by the official Church

Journeyman Skilled craftsman hired and paid by the day (from the French word *journée*, a day)

Lodge Workshop and shelter for masons on a building site

Manor Land belonging to a lord and usually farmed by the villeins who were his tenants

Masterpiece Fine example of their craft made by apprentices to qualify for the title 'mastercraftsman'

Mêlee Mock battle between two groups of armed men

Mercenary Hired soldier who fought for whoever paid the best

Moors Muslims from North Africa who dominated much of Spain and Portugal between the eighth and fifteenth centuries

Plainsong Type of church music common in medieval times

Portcullis Strong iron grating that could be lowered to block the entrance to a town or castle

Quill pen Pen made of a bird's feather, usually the wing feather of a goose

Ransom Sum of money demanded in exchange for the release of a prisoner

Reliquary Small casket or container in which sacred relics are kept

Scrip Small bag carried by pilgrims

Solar Small upper room in a castle used by the lord and his family

Surcoat Loose coat worn over armour, usually with the knight's coat-of-arms or emblem on it

Swaddling clothes Long strips of cloth which were used to wrap around babies

Tithe Payments made to the Church, usually a tenth of the crop

Troubadour Wandering poet and musician, especially popular in France

Villein Medieval peasant who farmed land for his landlord and was not a free man

Vizor Moveable faceguard on a helmet

Wattle and daub Twigs and branches covered with a plaster of mud or clay to make walls

Withy bands Binding made out of the strong, supple branches of the willow or osier

Some Important Dates

1066 Defeat of Harold of England at the Battle of Hastings by William, duke of Normandy, who becomes William I of England

1085–86 Domesday Book: the first ever survey of England and her people, made on the orders of William I

1099 The first crusade. The crusaders capture Jerusalem from the Muslims

1115 Founding of Clairvaux monastery by Bernard

1125 *History of England* written by William of Malmesbury

1132 London almost destroyed by fire

1132 First appearance of the Gothic style of arch in the church of Saint Denis, France

1139–53 Civil war in England between King Stephen and the Empress Matilda and their followers

c. 1150 The earliest papermills built in Spain

c. 1160 First modern windmills built in France

1170 The murder of Thomas à Becket in Canterbury cathedral

1174 Canterbury cathedral rebuilding begun, the first appearance of the Early English style of architecture

1191 First Lord Mayor of London appointed

1193 Richard I of England captured in Germany while returning from the crusades

1200 Coal being exported from Newcastle to the Continent

1211 Building of Rheims cathedral begins

1215 King John, under pressure from the nobles, signs Magna Carta restricting the power of the crown

1245–69 Westminster abbey is rebuilt in the Early English style of architecture

1265 Representatives of the chief towns of England summoned to attend the English Parliament for the first time

1312 Cross channel ferry service from Dover organised

1322 The octagon of Ely cathedral built, one of the finest examples of the Decorated style of architecture

1326 Earliest known picture of a European cannon

1337 Hundred Years' War between England and France begins

1346 Battle of Crécy, English forces defeated the French

1348–49 The Black Death at its peak in England

1350 Edward III passes Statute of Labourers in an attempt to fix wages

1381 The Peasants' Revolt

1387–90 Geoffrey Chaucer writes *The Canterbury Tales*

c. 1400 Beverley minster built, one of the greatest examples of the Perpendicular style of architecture

1415 English forces defeat the French at the Battle of Agincourt

1431 Joan of Arc burnt at the stake

1450 Paper made in England

1453 Hundred Years' War ends with the expulsion of the English from France, with the exception of Calais

1455 The Wars of the Roses begin

c. 1478 William Caxton sets up the first printing press in England at Westminster

1485 Battle of Bosworth ends the Wars of the Roses. Henry Tudor (Henry VII) defeats Richard III, becoming the first Tudor king

Index